Bug
JOURNAL

COPYRIGHT © NAOMI THUNDER, 2020

THIS BOOK BELONGS TO:

CONTACT INFORMATION	
NAME:	
ADDRESS:	
PHONE:	

START / END DATES

_____ / ___ / _____   TO   _____ / ___ / _____

BUG JOURNAL

DATE:	20.5.21	TIME: 3:-	SEASON:	○ SPRING ●SUMMER ○ FALL ○ WINTER
WEATHER CONDITIONS:		○ HOT ●WARM ○ SUNNY ●CLOUDY ○ RAINY ○ WINDY ○ FOGGY ○ COLD		
BUG NAME:	Worm			
WHERE DID YOU FIND IT?	Next to bug shed			
WHAT COLOR(S) IS THE BUG?	pink			
NUMBER OF LEGS?	none	DOES IT HAVE WINGS?	○ YES ●NO ○ NOT SURE	
NUMBER OF LEGS?	none			
THE BUG IS...	○ BIG ○ SHINY ○ FAST ○ SCARY ○ LITTLE ●SLOW ○ CUTE ○ ROUND ○ THIN			
DOES IT MAKE ANY SOUND?	○ YES ●NO	WAS IT ALONE OR IN A GROUP?	●ALONE ○ GROUP	

NOTES

the bug was wriggly

PHOTO/DRAWING

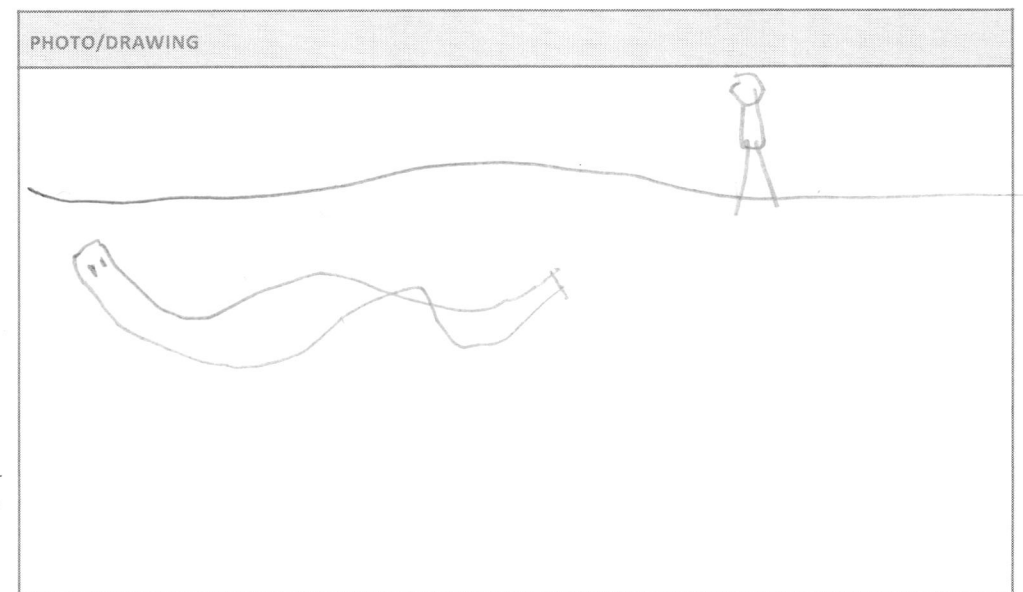

BUG JOURNAL

DATE:	20.6.21	TIME: 3:00	SEASON:	○ SPRING ●SUMMER ○ FALL ○ WINTER	
WEATHER CONDITIONS:		○ HOT ●WARM ○ SUNNY ●CLOUDY ○ RAINY ○ WINDY ○ FOGGY ○ COLD			
BUG NAME:		bumble-dor beetle			
WHERE DID YOU FIND IT?		next to the bug shed			
WHAT COLOR(S) IS THE BUG?		black			
NUMBER OF LEGS?	6	DOES IT HAVE WINGS?	●YES ○ NO ○ NOT SURE		
NUMBER OF LEGS?	6				
THE BUG IS…		○ BIG ○ SHINY ○ FAST ○ SCARY ○ LITTLE ○ SLOW ○ CUTE ●ROUND ○ THIN			
DOES IT MAKE ANY SOUND?		●YES ○ NO	WAS IT ALONE OR IN A GROUP?	●ALONE ○ GROUP	

NOTES

It is burry

PHOTO/DRAWING

BUG JOURNAL

DATE:		TIME:		SEASON:	○ SPRING ○ SUMMER ○ FALL ○ WINTER
WEATHER CONDITIONS:			○ HOT ○ WARM ○ SUNNY ○ CLOUDY ○ RAINY ○ WINDY ○ FOGGY ○ COLD
BUG NAME:					
WHERE DID YOU FIND IT?					
WHAT COLOR(S) IS THE BUG?					
NUMBER OF LEGS?		DOES IT HAVE WINGS?		○ YES ○ NO ○ NOT SURE	
NUMBER OF LEGS?					
THE BUG IS...		○ BIG ○ SHINY ○ FAST ○ SCARY ○ LITTLE ○ SLOW ○ CUTE ○ ROUND ○ THIN			
DOES IT MAKE ANY SOUND?	○ YES ○ NO	WAS IT ALONE OR IN A GROUP?		○ ALONE ○ GROUP	

NOTES

PHOTO/DRAWING

BUG JOURNAL

DATE:		TIME:		SEASON:	○ SPRING ○ SUMMER ○ FALL ○ WINTER
WEATHER CONDITIONS:			○ HOT ○ WARM ○ SUNNY ○ CLOUDY ○ RAINY ○ WINDY ○ FOGGY ○ COLD		
BUG NAME:					
WHERE DID YOU FIND IT?					
WHAT COLOR(S) IS THE BUG?					
NUMBER OF LEGS?			**DOES IT HAVE WINGS?**	○ YES ○ NO ○ NOT SURE	
NUMBER OF LEGS?					
THE BUG IS...		○ BIG ○ SHINY ○ FAST ○ SCARY ○ LITTLE ○ SLOW ○ CUTE ○ ROUND ○ THIN			
DOES IT MAKE ANY SOUND?	○ YES ○ NO		**WAS IT ALONE OR IN A GROUP?**	○ ALONE ○ GROUP	

NOTES

PHOTO/DRAWING

BUG JOURNAL

DATE:		TIME:		SEASON:	○ SPRING ○ SUMMER ○ FALL ○ WINTER
WEATHER CONDITIONS:		○ HOT ○ WARM ○ SUNNY ○ CLOUDY ○ RAINY ○ WINDY ○ FOGGY ○ COLD			
BUG NAME:					
WHERE DID YOU FIND IT?					
WHAT COLOR(S) IS THE BUG?					
NUMBER OF LEGS?		**DOES IT HAVE WINGS?**		○ YES ○ NO ○ NOT SURE	
NUMBER OF LEGS?					
THE BUG IS...	○ BIG ○ SHINY ○ FAST ○ SCARY ○ LITTLE ○ SLOW ○ CUTE ○ ROUND ○ THIN				
DOES IT MAKE ANY SOUND?	○ YES ○ NO	**WAS IT ALONE OR IN A GROUP?**		○ ALONE ○ GROUP	

NOTES

PHOTO/DRAWING

BUG JOURNAL

DATE:		TIME:		SEASON:	○ SPRING ○ SUMMER ○ FALL ○ WINTER	
WEATHER CONDITIONS:		○ HOT ○ WARM ○ SUNNY ○ CLOUDY ○ RAINY ○ WINDY ○ FOGGY ○ COLD				
BUG NAME:						
WHERE DID YOU FIND IT?						
WHAT COLOR(S) IS THE BUG?						
NUMBER OF LEGS?			DOES IT HAVE WINGS?		○ YES ○ NO ○ NOT SURE	
NUMBER OF LEGS?						
THE BUG IS…		○ BIG ○ SHINY ○ FAST ○ SCARY ○ LITTLE ○ SLOW ○ CUTE ○ ROUND ○ THIN				
DOES IT MAKE ANY SOUND?		○ YES ○ NO	WAS IT ALONE OR IN A GROUP?		○ ALONE ○ GROUP	

NOTES

PHOTO/DRAWING

BUG JOURNAL

DATE:		TIME:		SEASON:	○ SPRING ○ SUMMER ○ FALL ○ WINTER
WEATHER CONDITIONS:		○ HOT ○ WARM ○ SUNNY ○ CLOUDY ○ RAINY ○ WINDY ○ FOGGY ○ COLD			
BUG NAME:						
WHERE DID YOU FIND IT?						
WHAT COLOR(S) IS THE BUG?						
NUMBER OF LEGS?		**DOES IT HAVE WINGS?**		○ YES ○ NO ○ NOT SURE	
NUMBER OF LEGS?						
THE BUG IS…	○ BIG ○ SHINY ○ FAST ○ SCARY ○ LITTLE ○ SLOW ○ CUTE ○ ROUND ○ THIN				
DOES IT MAKE ANY SOUND?	○ YES ○ NO	**WAS IT ALONE OR IN A GROUP?**			○ ALONE ○ GROUP

NOTES

PHOTO/DRAWING

BUG JOURNAL

DATE:		TIME:		SEASON:	○ SPRING ○ SUMMER ○ FALL ○ WINTER
WEATHER CONDITIONS:			○ HOT ○ WARM ○ SUNNY ○ CLOUDY ○ RAINY ○ WINDY ○ FOGGY ○ COLD		
BUG NAME:					
WHERE DID YOU FIND IT?					
WHAT COLOR(S) IS THE BUG?					
NUMBER OF LEGS?		**DOES IT HAVE WINGS?**		○ YES ○ NO ○ NOT SURE	
NUMBER OF LEGS?					
THE BUG IS...		○ BIG ○ SHINY ○ FAST ○ SCARY ○ LITTLE ○ SLOW ○ CUTE ○ ROUND ○ THIN				
DOES IT MAKE ANY SOUND?	○ YES ○ NO	**WAS IT ALONE OR IN A GROUP?**		○ ALONE ○ GROUP	

NOTES

PHOTO/DRAWING

BUG JOURNAL

DATE:		TIME:		SEASON:	○ SPRING ○ SUMMER ○ FALL ○ WINTER	
WEATHER CONDITIONS:		○ HOT ○ WARM ○ SUNNY ○ CLOUDY ○ RAINY ○ WINDY ○ FOGGY ○ COLD				
BUG NAME:						
WHERE DID YOU FIND IT?						
WHAT COLOR(S) IS THE BUG?						
NUMBER OF LEGS?			DOES IT HAVE WINGS?		○ YES ○ NO ○ NOT SURE	
NUMBER OF LEGS?						
THE BUG IS...		○ BIG ○ SHINY ○ FAST ○ SCARY ○ LITTLE ○ SLOW ○ CUTE ○ ROUND ○ THIN				
DOES IT MAKE ANY SOUND?		○ YES ○ NO	WAS IT ALONE OR IN A GROUP?		○ ALONE ○ GROUP	

NOTES

PHOTO/DRAWING

BUG JOURNAL

DATE:		TIME:		SEASON:	○ SPRING ○ SUMMER ○ FALL ○ WINTER	
WEATHER CONDITIONS:		○ HOT ○ WARM ○ SUNNY ○ CLOUDY ○ RAINY ○ WINDY ○ FOGGY ○ COLD				
BUG NAME:						
WHERE DID YOU FIND IT?						
WHAT COLOR(S) IS THE BUG?						
NUMBER OF LEGS?			DOES IT HAVE WINGS?		○ YES ○ NO ○ NOT SURE	
NUMBER OF LEGS?						
THE BUG IS...		○ BIG ○ SHINY ○ FAST ○ SCARY ○ LITTLE ○ SLOW ○ CUTE ○ ROUND ○ THIN				
DOES IT MAKE ANY SOUND?		○ YES ○ NO	WAS IT ALONE OR IN A GROUP?		○ ALONE ○ GROUP	

NOTES

PHOTO/DRAWING

BUG JOURNAL

DATE:		TIME:		SEASON:	○ SPRING ○ SUMMER ○ FALL ○ WINTER
WEATHER CONDITIONS:			○ HOT ○ WARM ○ SUNNY ○ CLOUDY ○ RAINY ○ WINDY ○ FOGGY ○ COLD			
BUG NAME:					
WHERE DID YOU FIND IT?					
WHAT COLOR(S) IS THE BUG?					
NUMBER OF LEGS?			DOES IT HAVE WINGS?	○ YES ○ NO ○ NOT SURE	
NUMBER OF LEGS?					
THE BUG IS...	○ BIG ○ SHINY ○ FAST ○ SCARY ○ LITTLE ○ SLOW ○ CUTE ○ ROUND ○ THIN				
DOES IT MAKE ANY SOUND?	○ YES ○ NO		WAS IT ALONE OR IN A GROUP?	○ ALONE ○ GROUP	

NOTES

PHOTO/DRAWING

BUG JOURNAL

DATE:		TIME:		SEASON:	○ SPRING ○ SUMMER ○ FALL ○ WINTER	
WEATHER CONDITIONS:		○ HOT ○ WARM ○ SUNNY ○ CLOUDY ○ RAINY ○ WINDY ○ FOGGY ○ COLD				
BUG NAME:						
WHERE DID YOU FIND IT?						
WHAT COLOR(S) IS THE BUG?						
NUMBER OF LEGS?			DOES IT HAVE WINGS?		○ YES ○ NO ○ NOT SURE	
NUMBER OF LEGS?						
THE BUG IS...		○ BIG ○ SHINY ○ FAST ○ SCARY ○ LITTLE ○ SLOW ○ CUTE ○ ROUND ○ THIN				
DOES IT MAKE ANY SOUND?		○ YES ○ NO	WAS IT ALONE OR IN A GROUP?		○ ALONE ○ GROUP	

NOTES

PHOTO/DRAWING

BUG JOURNAL

DATE:		TIME:		SEASON:	○ SPRING ○ SUMMER ○ FALL ○ WINTER
WEATHER CONDITIONS:		○ HOT ○ WARM ○ SUNNY ○ CLOUDY ○ RAINY ○ WINDY ○ FOGGY ○ COLD
BUG NAME:		
WHERE DID YOU FIND IT?		
WHAT COLOR(S) IS THE BUG?		
NUMBER OF LEGS?		DOES IT HAVE WINGS?	○ YES ○ NO ○ NOT SURE
NUMBER OF LEGS?		
THE BUG IS...		○ BIG ○ SHINY ○ FAST ○ SCARY ○ LITTLE ○ SLOW ○ CUTE ○ ROUND ○ THIN
DOES IT MAKE ANY SOUND?	○ YES ○ NO	WAS IT ALONE OR IN A GROUP?	○ ALONE ○ GROUP

NOTES

PHOTO/DRAWING

BUG JOURNAL

DATE:		TIME:		SEASON:	○ SPRING ○ SUMMER ○ FALL ○ WINTER
WEATHER CONDITIONS:		○ HOT ○ WARM ○ SUNNY ○ CLOUDY ○ RAINY ○ WINDY ○ FOGGY ○ COLD			
BUG NAME:					
WHERE DID YOU FIND IT?					
WHAT COLOR(S) IS THE BUG?					
NUMBER OF LEGS?		**DOES IT HAVE WINGS?**		○ YES ○ NO ○ NOT SURE	
NUMBER OF LEGS?					
THE BUG IS...	○ BIG ○ SHINY ○ FAST ○ SCARY ○ LITTLE ○ SLOW ○ CUTE ○ ROUND ○ THIN				
DOES IT MAKE ANY SOUND?	○ YES ○ NO	**WAS IT ALONE OR IN A GROUP?**		○ ALONE ○ GROUP	

NOTES

PHOTO/DRAWING

BUG JOURNAL

DATE:		TIME:		SEASON:	○ SPRING ○ SUMMER ○ FALL ○ WINTER	
WEATHER CONDITIONS:		○ HOT ○ WARM ○ SUNNY ○ CLOUDY ○ RAINY ○ WINDY ○ FOGGY ○ COLD				
BUG NAME:						
WHERE DID YOU FIND IT?						
WHAT COLOR(S) IS THE BUG?						
NUMBER OF LEGS?			DOES IT HAVE WINGS?		○ YES ○ NO ○ NOT SURE	
NUMBER OF LEGS?						
THE BUG IS...		○ BIG ○ SHINY ○ FAST ○ SCARY ○ LITTLE ○ SLOW ○ CUTE ○ ROUND ○ THIN				
DOES IT MAKE ANY SOUND?		○ YES ○ NO	WAS IT ALONE OR IN A GROUP?		○ ALONE ○ GROUP	

NOTES

PHOTO/DRAWING

BUG JOURNAL

DATE:		TIME:		SEASON:	○ SPRING ○ SUMMER ○ FALL ○ WINTER	
WEATHER CONDITIONS:		○ HOT ○ WARM ○ SUNNY ○ CLOUDY ○ RAINY ○ WINDY ○ FOGGY ○ COLD				
BUG NAME:						
WHERE DID YOU FIND IT?						
WHAT COLOR(S) IS THE BUG?						
NUMBER OF LEGS?			DOES IT HAVE WINGS?		○ YES ○ NO ○ NOT SURE	
NUMBER OF LEGS?						
THE BUG IS...		○ BIG ○ SHINY ○ FAST ○ SCARY ○ LITTLE ○ SLOW ○ CUTE ○ ROUND ○ THIN				
DOES IT MAKE ANY SOUND?		○ YES ○ NO	WAS IT ALONE OR IN A GROUP?		○ ALONE ○ GROUP	

NOTES

PHOTO/DRAWING

BUG JOURNAL

DATE:		TIME:		SEASON:	○ SPRING ○ SUMMER ○ FALL ○ WINTER
WEATHER CONDITIONS:		○ HOT ○ WARM ○ SUNNY ○ CLOUDY ○ RAINY ○ WINDY ○ FOGGY ○ COLD			
BUG NAME:					
WHERE DID YOU FIND IT?					
WHAT COLOR(S) IS THE BUG?					
NUMBER OF LEGS?		**DOES IT HAVE WINGS?**		○ YES ○ NO ○ NOT SURE	
NUMBER OF LEGS?					
THE BUG IS...	○ BIG ○ SHINY ○ FAST ○ SCARY ○ LITTLE ○ SLOW ○ CUTE ○ ROUND ○ THIN				
DOES IT MAKE ANY SOUND?	○ YES ○ NO	**WAS IT ALONE OR IN A GROUP?**		○ ALONE ○ GROUP	

NOTES

PHOTO/DRAWING

BUG JOURNAL

DATE:		TIME:		SEASON:	○ SPRING ○ SUMMER ○ FALL ○ WINTER
WEATHER CONDITIONS:			○ HOT ○ WARM ○ SUNNY ○ CLOUDY ○ RAINY ○ WINDY ○ FOGGY ○ COLD
BUG NAME:					
WHERE DID YOU FIND IT?					
WHAT COLOR(S) IS THE BUG?					
NUMBER OF LEGS?			**DOES IT HAVE WINGS?**		○ YES ○ NO ○ NOT SURE
NUMBER OF LEGS?					
THE BUG IS...			○ BIG ○ SHINY ○ FAST ○ SCARY ○ LITTLE ○ SLOW ○ CUTE ○ ROUND ○ THIN
DOES IT MAKE ANY SOUND?		○ YES ○ NO	**WAS IT ALONE OR IN A GROUP?**		○ ALONE ○ GROUP

NOTES

PHOTO/DRAWING

BUG JOURNAL

DATE:		TIME:		SEASON:	○ SPRING ○ SUMMER ○ FALL ○ WINTER
WEATHER CONDITIONS:			○ HOT ○ WARM ○ SUNNY ○ CLOUDY ○ RAINY ○ WINDY ○ FOGGY ○ COLD		
BUG NAME:					
WHERE DID YOU FIND IT?					
WHAT COLOR(S) IS THE BUG?					
NUMBER OF LEGS?		**DOES IT HAVE WINGS?**		○ YES ○ NO ○ NOT SURE	
NUMBER OF LEGS?					
THE BUG IS...		○ BIG ○ SHINY ○ FAST ○ SCARY ○ LITTLE ○ SLOW ○ CUTE ○ ROUND ○ THIN			
DOES IT MAKE ANY SOUND?	○ YES ○ NO	**WAS IT ALONE OR IN A GROUP?**		○ ALONE ○ GROUP	

NOTES

PHOTO/DRAWING

BUG JOURNAL

DATE:		TIME:		SEASON:	○ SPRING ○ SUMMER ○ FALL ○ WINTER	
WEATHER CONDITIONS:		○ HOT ○ WARM ○ SUNNY ○ CLOUDY ○ RAINY ○ WINDY ○ FOGGY ○ COLD				
BUG NAME:						
WHERE DID YOU FIND IT?						
WHAT COLOR(S) IS THE BUG?						
NUMBER OF LEGS?			DOES IT HAVE WINGS?		○ YES ○ NO ○ NOT SURE	
NUMBER OF LEGS?						
THE BUG IS...		○ BIG ○ SHINY ○ FAST ○ SCARY ○ LITTLE ○ SLOW ○ CUTE ○ ROUND ○ THIN				
DOES IT MAKE ANY SOUND?		○ YES ○ NO	WAS IT ALONE OR IN A GROUP?		○ ALONE ○ GROUP	

NOTES

PHOTO/DRAWING

BUG JOURNAL

DATE:		TIME:		SEASON:	○ SPRING ○ SUMMER ○ FALL ○ WINTER
WEATHER CONDITIONS:			○ HOT ○ WARM ○ SUNNY ○ CLOUDY ○ RAINY ○ WINDY ○ FOGGY ○ COLD		
BUG NAME:					
WHERE DID YOU FIND IT?					
WHAT COLOR(S) IS THE BUG?					
NUMBER OF LEGS?			**DOES IT HAVE WINGS?**		○ YES ○ NO ○ NOT SURE
NUMBER OF LEGS?					
THE BUG IS...			○ BIG ○ SHINY ○ FAST ○ SCARY ○ LITTLE ○ SLOW ○ CUTE ○ ROUND ○ THIN		
DOES IT MAKE ANY SOUND?		○ YES ○ NO	**WAS IT ALONE OR IN A GROUP?**		○ ALONE ○ GROUP

NOTES

PHOTO/DRAWING

BUG JOURNAL

DATE:		TIME:		SEASON:	○ SPRING ○ SUMMER ○ FALL ○ WINTER
WEATHER CONDITIONS:			○ HOT ○ WARM ○ SUNNY ○ CLOUDY ○ RAINY ○ WINDY ○ FOGGY ○ COLD

BUG NAME:	
WHERE DID YOU FIND IT?	
WHAT COLOR(S) IS THE BUG?	

NUMBER OF LEGS?		DOES IT HAVE WINGS?	○ YES ○ NO ○ NOT SURE
NUMBER OF LEGS?			
THE BUG IS...		○ BIG ○ SHINY ○ FAST ○ SCARY ○ LITTLE ○ SLOW ○ CUTE ○ ROUND ○ THIN	
DOES IT MAKE ANY SOUND?	○ YES ○ NO	WAS IT ALONE OR IN A GROUP?	○ ALONE ○ GROUP

NOTES

PHOTO/DRAWING

BUG JOURNAL

DATE:		TIME:		SEASON:	○ SPRING ○ SUMMER ○ FALL ○ WINTER	
WEATHER CONDITIONS:		○ HOT ○ WARM ○ SUNNY ○ CLOUDY ○ RAINY ○ WINDY ○ FOGGY ○ COLD
BUG NAME:						
WHERE DID YOU FIND IT?						
WHAT COLOR(S) IS THE BUG?						
NUMBER OF LEGS?			DOES IT HAVE WINGS?		○ YES ○ NO ○ NOT SURE	
NUMBER OF LEGS?						
THE BUG IS...		○ BIG ○ SHINY ○ FAST ○ SCARY ○ LITTLE ○ SLOW ○ CUTE ○ ROUND ○ THIN				
DOES IT MAKE ANY SOUND?		○ YES ○ NO	WAS IT ALONE OR IN A GROUP?		○ ALONE ○ GROUP	

NOTES

PHOTO/DRAWING

BUG JOURNAL

DATE:		TIME:		SEASON:	○ SPRING ○ SUMMER ○ FALL ○ WINTER
WEATHER CONDITIONS:		○ HOT ○ WARM ○ SUNNY ○ CLOUDY ○ RAINY ○ WINDY ○ FOGGY ○ COLD			
BUG NAME:					
WHERE DID YOU FIND IT?					
WHAT COLOR(S) IS THE BUG?					
NUMBER OF LEGS?			**DOES IT HAVE WINGS?**		○ YES ○ NO ○ NOT SURE
NUMBER OF LEGS?					
THE BUG IS...		○ BIG ○ SHINY ○ FAST ○ SCARY ○ LITTLE ○ SLOW ○ CUTE ○ ROUND ○ THIN			
DOES IT MAKE ANY SOUND?		○ YES ○ NO	**WAS IT ALONE OR IN A GROUP?**		○ ALONE ○ GROUP

NOTES

PHOTO/DRAWING

BUG JOURNAL

DATE:		TIME:		SEASON:	○ SPRING ○ SUMMER ○ FALL ○ WINTER	
WEATHER CONDITIONS:		○ HOT ○ WARM ○ SUNNY ○ CLOUDY ○ RAINY ○ WINDY ○ FOGGY ○ COLD				
BUG NAME:						
WHERE DID YOU FIND IT?						
WHAT COLOR(S) IS THE BUG?						
NUMBER OF LEGS?			DOES IT HAVE WINGS?		○ YES ○ NO ○ NOT SURE	
NUMBER OF LEGS?						
THE BUG IS...		○ BIG ○ SHINY ○ FAST ○ SCARY ○ LITTLE ○ SLOW ○ CUTE ○ ROUND ○ THIN				
DOES IT MAKE ANY SOUND?		○ YES ○ NO	WAS IT ALONE OR IN A GROUP?		○ ALONE ○ GROUP	

NOTES

PHOTO/DRAWING

BUG JOURNAL

DATE:		TIME:		SEASON:	○ SPRING ○ SUMMER ○ FALL ○ WINTER
WEATHER CONDITIONS:			○ HOT ○ WARM ○ SUNNY ○ CLOUDY ○ RAINY ○ WINDY ○ FOGGY ○ COLD		
BUG NAME:					
WHERE DID YOU FIND IT?					
WHAT COLOR(S) IS THE BUG?					
NUMBER OF LEGS?			DOES IT HAVE WINGS?	○ YES ○ NO ○ NOT SURE	
NUMBER OF LEGS?					
THE BUG IS…		○ BIG ○ SHINY ○ FAST ○ SCARY ○ LITTLE ○ SLOW ○ CUTE ○ ROUND ○ THIN			
DOES IT MAKE ANY SOUND?	○ YES ○ NO	WAS IT ALONE OR IN A GROUP?		○ ALONE ○ GROUP	

NOTES

PHOTO/DRAWING

BUG JOURNAL

DATE:		TIME:	SEASON:	○ SPRING ○ SUMMER ○ FALL ○ WINTER

WEATHER CONDITIONS:	○ HOT ○ WARM ○ SUNNY ○ CLOUDY ○ RAINY ○ WINDY ○ FOGGY ○ COLD
BUG NAME:	
WHERE DID YOU FIND IT?	
WHAT COLOR(S) IS THE BUG?	
NUMBER OF LEGS?	DOES IT HAVE WINGS? ○ YES ○ NO ○ NOT SURE
NUMBER OF LEGS?	
THE BUG IS...	○ BIG ○ SHINY ○ FAST ○ SCARY ○ LITTLE ○ SLOW ○ CUTE ○ ROUND ○ THIN
DOES IT MAKE ANY SOUND?	○ YES ○ NO WAS IT ALONE OR IN A GROUP? ○ ALONE ○ GROUP

NOTES

PHOTO/DRAWING

BUG JOURNAL

DATE:		TIME:		SEASON:	○ SPRING ○ SUMMER ○ FALL ○ WINTER	
WEATHER CONDITIONS:		○ HOT ○ WARM ○ SUNNY ○ CLOUDY ○ RAINY ○ WINDY ○ FOGGY ○ COLD				
BUG NAME:						
WHERE DID YOU FIND IT?						
WHAT COLOR(S) IS THE BUG?						
NUMBER OF LEGS?			DOES IT HAVE WINGS?		○ YES ○ NO ○ NOT SURE	
NUMBER OF LEGS?						
THE BUG IS...		○ BIG ○ SHINY ○ FAST ○ SCARY ○ LITTLE ○ SLOW ○ CUTE ○ ROUND ○ THIN				
DOES IT MAKE ANY SOUND?		○ YES ○ NO	WAS IT ALONE OR IN A GROUP?		○ ALONE ○ GROUP	

NOTES

PHOTO/DRAWING

BUG JOURNAL

DATE:		TIME:		SEASON:	○ SPRING ○ SUMMER ○ FALL ○ WINTER

WEATHER CONDITIONS:	○ HOT ○ WARM ○ SUNNY ○ CLOUDY ○ RAINY ○ WINDY ○ FOGGY ○ COLD
BUG NAME:	
WHERE DID YOU FIND IT?	
WHAT COLOR(S) IS THE BUG?	

NUMBER OF LEGS?		DOES IT HAVE WINGS?	○ YES ○ NO ○ NOT SURE
NUMBER OF LEGS?			

THE BUG IS...	○ BIG ○ SHINY ○ FAST ○ SCARY ○ LITTLE ○ SLOW ○ CUTE ○ ROUND ○ THIN
DOES IT MAKE ANY SOUND? ○ YES ○ NO	WAS IT ALONE OR IN A GROUP? ○ ALONE ○ GROUP

NOTES

PHOTO/DRAWING

BUG JOURNAL

DATE:		TIME:		SEASON:	○ SPRING ○ SUMMER ○ FALL ○ WINTER	
WEATHER CONDITIONS:		○ HOT ○ WARM ○ SUNNY ○ CLOUDY ○ RAINY ○ WINDY ○ FOGGY ○ COLD				
BUG NAME:						
WHERE DID YOU FIND IT?						
WHAT COLOR(S) IS THE BUG?						
NUMBER OF LEGS?			DOES IT HAVE WINGS?		○ YES ○ NO ○ NOT SURE	
NUMBER OF LEGS?						
THE BUG IS…		○ BIG ○ SHINY ○ FAST ○ SCARY ○ LITTLE ○ SLOW ○ CUTE ○ ROUND ○ THIN				
DOES IT MAKE ANY SOUND?		○ YES ○ NO	WAS IT ALONE OR IN A GROUP?		○ ALONE ○ GROUP	

NOTES

PHOTO/DRAWING

BUG JOURNAL

DATE:		TIME:		SEASON:	○ SPRING ○ SUMMER ○ FALL ○ WINTER
WEATHER CONDITIONS:			○ HOT ○ WARM ○ SUNNY ○ CLOUDY ○ RAINY ○ WINDY ○ FOGGY ○ COLD		
BUG NAME:					
WHERE DID YOU FIND IT?					
WHAT COLOR(S) IS THE BUG?					
NUMBER OF LEGS?			**DOES IT HAVE WINGS?**	○ YES ○ NO ○ NOT SURE	
NUMBER OF LEGS?					
THE BUG IS...		○ BIG ○ SHINY ○ FAST ○ SCARY ○ LITTLE ○ SLOW ○ CUTE ○ ROUND ○ THIN			
DOES IT MAKE ANY SOUND?	○ YES ○ NO		**WAS IT ALONE OR IN A GROUP?**	○ ALONE ○ GROUP	

NOTES

PHOTO/DRAWING

BUG JOURNAL

DATE:		TIME:		SEASON:	○ SPRING ○ SUMMER ○ FALL ○ WINTER
WEATHER CONDITIONS:			○ HOT ○ WARM ○ SUNNY ○ CLOUDY ○ RAINY ○ WINDY ○ FOGGY ○ COLD		
BUG NAME:					
WHERE DID YOU FIND IT?					
WHAT COLOR(S) IS THE BUG?					
NUMBER OF LEGS?		**DOES IT HAVE WINGS?**		○ YES ○ NO ○ NOT SURE	
NUMBER OF LEGS?					
THE BUG IS...		○ BIG ○ SHINY ○ FAST ○ SCARY ○ LITTLE ○ SLOW ○ CUTE ○ ROUND ○ THIN			
DOES IT MAKE ANY SOUND?	○ YES ○ NO	**WAS IT ALONE OR IN A GROUP?**		○ ALONE ○ GROUP	

NOTES

PHOTO/DRAWING

BUG JOURNAL

DATE:		TIME:		SEASON:	○ SPRING ○ SUMMER ○ FALL ○ WINTER
WEATHER CONDITIONS:		○ HOT ○ WARM ○ SUNNY ○ CLOUDY ○ RAINY ○ WINDY ○ FOGGY ○ COLD			
BUG NAME:					
WHERE DID YOU FIND IT?					
WHAT COLOR(S) IS THE BUG?					
NUMBER OF LEGS?		**DOES IT HAVE WINGS?**		○ YES ○ NO ○ NOT SURE	
NUMBER OF LEGS?					
THE BUG IS...	○ BIG ○ SHINY ○ FAST ○ SCARY ○ LITTLE ○ SLOW ○ CUTE ○ ROUND ○ THIN				
DOES IT MAKE ANY SOUND?	○ YES ○ NO	**WAS IT ALONE OR IN A GROUP?**			○ ALONE ○ GROUP

NOTES

PHOTO/DRAWING

BUG JOURNAL

DATE:		TIME:		SEASON:	○ SPRING ○ SUMMER ○ FALL ○ WINTER
WEATHER CONDITIONS:		○ HOT ○ WARM ○ SUNNY ○ CLOUDY ○ RAINY ○ WINDY ○ FOGGY ○ COLD			
BUG NAME:					
WHERE DID YOU FIND IT?					
WHAT COLOR(S) IS THE BUG?					
NUMBER OF LEGS?		**DOES IT HAVE WINGS?**		○ YES ○ NO ○ NOT SURE	
NUMBER OF LEGS?					
THE BUG IS...		○ BIG ○ SHINY ○ FAST ○ SCARY ○ LITTLE ○ SLOW ○ CUTE ○ ROUND ○ THIN			
DOES IT MAKE ANY SOUND?	○ YES ○ NO	**WAS IT ALONE OR IN A GROUP?**		○ ALONE ○ GROUP	

NOTES

PHOTO/DRAWING

BUG JOURNAL

DATE:		TIME:		SEASON:	○ SPRING ○ SUMMER ○ FALL ○ WINTER
WEATHER CONDITIONS:		○ HOT ○ WARM ○ SUNNY ○ CLOUDY ○ RAINY ○ WINDY ○ FOGGY ○ COLD			
BUG NAME:					
WHERE DID YOU FIND IT?					
WHAT COLOR(S) IS THE BUG?					
NUMBER OF LEGS?			**DOES IT HAVE WINGS?**		○ YES ○ NO ○ NOT SURE
NUMBER OF LEGS?					
THE BUG IS...		○ BIG ○ SHINY ○ FAST ○ SCARY ○ LITTLE ○ SLOW ○ CUTE ○ ROUND ○ THIN			
DOES IT MAKE ANY SOUND?		○ YES ○ NO	**WAS IT ALONE OR IN A GROUP?**		○ ALONE ○ GROUP

NOTES

PHOTO/DRAWING

BUG JOURNAL

DATE:		TIME:		SEASON:	○ SPRING ○ SUMMER ○ FALL ○ WINTER	
WEATHER CONDITIONS:		○ HOT ○ WARM ○ SUNNY ○ CLOUDY ○ RAINY ○ WINDY ○ FOGGY ○ COLD				
BUG NAME:						
WHERE DID YOU FIND IT?						
WHAT COLOR(S) IS THE BUG?						
NUMBER OF LEGS?			DOES IT HAVE WINGS?	○ YES ○ NO ○ NOT SURE		
NUMBER OF LEGS?						
THE BUG IS...		○ BIG ○ SHINY ○ FAST ○ SCARY ○ LITTLE ○ SLOW ○ CUTE ○ ROUND ○ THIN				
DOES IT MAKE ANY SOUND?	○ YES ○ NO		WAS IT ALONE OR IN A GROUP?	○ ALONE ○ GROUP		

NOTES

PHOTO/DRAWING

BUG JOURNAL

DATE:		TIME:		SEASON:	○ SPRING ○ SUMMER ○ FALL ○ WINTER	
WEATHER CONDITIONS:		○ HOT ○ WARM ○ SUNNY ○ CLOUDY ○ RAINY ○ WINDY ○ FOGGY ○ COLD				
BUG NAME:						
WHERE DID YOU FIND IT?						
WHAT COLOR(S) IS THE BUG?						
NUMBER OF LEGS?			DOES IT HAVE WINGS?		○ YES ○ NO ○ NOT SURE	
NUMBER OF LEGS?						
THE BUG IS...		○ BIG ○ SHINY ○ FAST ○ SCARY ○ LITTLE ○ SLOW ○ CUTE ○ ROUND ○ THIN				
DOES IT MAKE ANY SOUND?		○ YES ○ NO	WAS IT ALONE OR IN A GROUP?		○ ALONE ○ GROUP	

NOTES

PHOTO/DRAWING

BUG JOURNAL

DATE:		TIME:		SEASON:	○ SPRING ○ SUMMER ○ FALL ○ WINTER	
WEATHER CONDITIONS:		○ HOT ○ WARM ○ SUNNY ○ CLOUDY ○ RAINY ○ WINDY ○ FOGGY ○ COLD				
BUG NAME:						
WHERE DID YOU FIND IT?						
WHAT COLOR(S) IS THE BUG?						
NUMBER OF LEGS?			DOES IT HAVE WINGS?		○ YES ○ NO ○ NOT SURE	
NUMBER OF LEGS?						
THE BUG IS…		○ BIG ○ SHINY ○ FAST ○ SCARY ○ LITTLE ○ SLOW ○ CUTE ○ ROUND ○ THIN				
DOES IT MAKE ANY SOUND?		○ YES ○ NO	WAS IT ALONE OR IN A GROUP?		○ ALONE ○ GROUP	

NOTES

PHOTO/DRAWING

BUG JOURNAL

DATE:		TIME:		SEASON:	○ SPRING ○ SUMMER ○ FALL ○ WINTER
WEATHER CONDITIONS:		○ HOT ○ WARM ○ SUNNY ○ CLOUDY ○ RAINY ○ WINDY ○ FOGGY ○ COLD			
BUG NAME:					
WHERE DID YOU FIND IT?					
WHAT COLOR(S) IS THE BUG?					
NUMBER OF LEGS?		**DOES IT HAVE WINGS?**		○ YES ○ NO ○ NOT SURE	
NUMBER OF LEGS?					
THE BUG IS…	○ BIG ○ SHINY ○ FAST ○ SCARY ○ LITTLE ○ SLOW ○ CUTE ○ ROUND ○ THIN				
DOES IT MAKE ANY SOUND?	○ YES ○ NO	**WAS IT ALONE OR IN A GROUP?**			○ ALONE ○ GROUP

NOTES

PHOTO/DRAWING

BUG JOURNAL

DATE:		TIME:		SEASON:	○ SPRING ○ SUMMER ○ FALL ○ WINTER	
WEATHER CONDITIONS:		○ HOT ○ WARM ○ SUNNY ○ CLOUDY ○ RAINY ○ WINDY ○ FOGGY ○ COLD				
BUG NAME:						
WHERE DID YOU FIND IT?						
WHAT COLOR(S) IS THE BUG?						
NUMBER OF LEGS?			DOES IT HAVE WINGS?		○ YES ○ NO ○ NOT SURE	
NUMBER OF LEGS?						
THE BUG IS...		○ BIG ○ SHINY ○ FAST ○ SCARY ○ LITTLE ○ SLOW ○ CUTE ○ ROUND ○ THIN				
DOES IT MAKE ANY SOUND?		○ YES ○ NO	WAS IT ALONE OR IN A GROUP?		○ ALONE ○ GROUP	

NOTES

PHOTO/DRAWING

BUG JOURNAL

DATE:		TIME:		SEASON:	○ SPRING ○ SUMMER ○ FALL ○ WINTER
WEATHER CONDITIONS:			○ HOT ○ WARM ○ SUNNY ○ CLOUDY ○ RAINY ○ WINDY ○ FOGGY ○ COLD
BUG NAME:					
WHERE DID YOU FIND IT?					
WHAT COLOR(S) IS THE BUG?					
NUMBER OF LEGS?			**DOES IT HAVE WINGS?**	○ YES ○ NO ○ NOT SURE	
NUMBER OF LEGS?					
THE BUG IS...		○ BIG ○ SHINY ○ FAST ○ SCARY ○ LITTLE ○ SLOW ○ CUTE ○ ROUND ○ THIN
DOES IT MAKE ANY SOUND?	○ YES ○ NO		**WAS IT ALONE OR IN A GROUP?**	○ ALONE ○ GROUP	

NOTES

PHOTO/DRAWING

BUG JOURNAL

DATE:		TIME:		SEASON:	○ SPRING ○ SUMMER ○ FALL ○ WINTER	
WEATHER CONDITIONS:		○ HOT ○ WARM ○ SUNNY ○ CLOUDY ○ RAINY ○ WINDY ○ FOGGY ○ COLD				
BUG NAME:						
WHERE DID YOU FIND IT?						
WHAT COLOR(S) IS THE BUG?						
NUMBER OF LEGS?			DOES IT HAVE WINGS?		○ YES ○ NO ○ NOT SURE	
NUMBER OF LEGS?						
THE BUG IS...		○ BIG ○ SHINY ○ FAST ○ SCARY ○ LITTLE ○ SLOW ○ CUTE ○ ROUND ○ THIN				
DOES IT MAKE ANY SOUND?		○ YES ○ NO	WAS IT ALONE OR IN A GROUP?		○ ALONE ○ GROUP	

NOTES

PHOTO/DRAWING

BUG JOURNAL

DATE:		TIME:		SEASON:	○ SPRING ○ SUMMER ○ FALL ○ WINTER
WEATHER CONDITIONS:			○ HOT ○ WARM ○ SUNNY ○ CLOUDY ○ RAINY ○ WINDY ○ FOGGY ○ COLD
BUG NAME:					
WHERE DID YOU FIND IT?					
WHAT COLOR(S) IS THE BUG?					
NUMBER OF LEGS?			**DOES IT HAVE WINGS?**		○ YES ○ NO ○ NOT SURE
NUMBER OF LEGS?					
THE BUG IS...			○ BIG ○ SHINY ○ FAST ○ SCARY ○ LITTLE ○ SLOW ○ CUTE ○ ROUND ○ THIN
DOES IT MAKE ANY SOUND?		○ YES ○ NO	**WAS IT ALONE OR IN A GROUP?**		○ ALONE ○ GROUP

NOTES

PHOTO/DRAWING

BUG JOURNAL

DATE:		TIME:		SEASON:	○ SPRING ○ SUMMER ○ FALL ○ WINTER
WEATHER CONDITIONS:		○ HOT ○ WARM ○ SUNNY ○ CLOUDY ○ RAINY ○ WINDY ○ FOGGY ○ COLD
BUG NAME:					
WHERE DID YOU FIND IT?					
WHAT COLOR(S) IS THE BUG?					
NUMBER OF LEGS?		**DOES IT HAVE WINGS?**		○ YES ○ NO ○ NOT SURE	
NUMBER OF LEGS?					
THE BUG IS...		○ BIG ○ SHINY ○ FAST ○ SCARY ○ LITTLE ○ SLOW ○ CUTE ○ ROUND ○ THIN			
DOES IT MAKE ANY SOUND?	○ YES ○ NO	**WAS IT ALONE OR IN A GROUP?**		○ ALONE ○ GROUP	

NOTES

PHOTO/DRAWING

BUG JOURNAL

DATE:		TIME:		SEASON:	○ SPRING ○ SUMMER ○ FALL ○ WINTER	
WEATHER CONDITIONS:		○ HOT ○ WARM ○ SUNNY ○ CLOUDY ○ RAINY ○ WINDY ○ FOGGY ○ COLD				
BUG NAME:						
WHERE DID YOU FIND IT?						
WHAT COLOR(S) IS THE BUG?						
NUMBER OF LEGS?			DOES IT HAVE WINGS?		○ YES ○ NO ○ NOT SURE	
NUMBER OF LEGS?						
THE BUG IS...		○ BIG ○ SHINY ○ FAST ○ SCARY ○ LITTLE ○ SLOW ○ CUTE ○ ROUND ○ THIN				
DOES IT MAKE ANY SOUND?		○ YES ○ NO	WAS IT ALONE OR IN A GROUP?		○ ALONE ○ GROUP	

NOTES

PHOTO/DRAWING

BUG JOURNAL

DATE:		TIME:		SEASON:	○ SPRING ○ SUMMER ○ FALL ○ WINTER	
WEATHER CONDITIONS:		○ HOT ○ WARM ○ SUNNY ○ CLOUDY ○ RAINY ○ WINDY ○ FOGGY ○ COLD				
BUG NAME:						
WHERE DID YOU FIND IT?						
WHAT COLOR(S) IS THE BUG?						
NUMBER OF LEGS?			DOES IT HAVE WINGS?		○ YES ○ NO ○ NOT SURE	
NUMBER OF LEGS?						
THE BUG IS...		○ BIG ○ SHINY ○ FAST ○ SCARY ○ LITTLE ○ SLOW ○ CUTE ○ ROUND ○ THIN				
DOES IT MAKE ANY SOUND?		○ YES ○ NO	WAS IT ALONE OR IN A GROUP?		○ ALONE ○ GROUP	

NOTES

PHOTO/DRAWING

BUG JOURNAL

DATE:		TIME:		SEASON:	○ SPRING ○ SUMMER ○ FALL ○ WINTER

WEATHER CONDITIONS:	○ HOT ○ WARM ○ SUNNY ○ CLOUDY ○ RAINY ○ WINDY ○ FOGGY ○ COLD
BUG NAME:	
WHERE DID YOU FIND IT?	
WHAT COLOR(S) IS THE BUG?	
NUMBER OF LEGS?		DOES IT HAVE WINGS?	○ YES ○ NO ○ NOT SURE
NUMBER OF LEGS?	
THE BUG IS…	○ BIG ○ SHINY ○ FAST ○ SCARY ○ LITTLE ○ SLOW ○ CUTE ○ ROUND ○ THIN
DOES IT MAKE ANY SOUND?	○ YES ○ NO	WAS IT ALONE OR IN A GROUP?	○ ALONE ○ GROUP

NOTES

PHOTO/DRAWING

BUG JOURNAL

DATE:		TIME:		SEASON:	○ SPRING ○ SUMMER ○ FALL ○ WINTER	
WEATHER CONDITIONS:		○ HOT ○ WARM ○ SUNNY ○ CLOUDY ○ RAINY ○ WINDY ○ FOGGY ○ COLD				
BUG NAME:						
WHERE DID YOU FIND IT?						
WHAT COLOR(S) IS THE BUG?						
NUMBER OF LEGS?			DOES IT HAVE WINGS?		○ YES ○ NO ○ NOT SURE	
NUMBER OF LEGS?						
THE BUG IS…		○ BIG ○ SHINY ○ FAST ○ SCARY ○ LITTLE ○ SLOW ○ CUTE ○ ROUND ○ THIN				
DOES IT MAKE ANY SOUND?		○ YES ○ NO	WAS IT ALONE OR IN A GROUP?		○ ALONE ○ GROUP	

NOTES

PHOTO/DRAWING

BUG JOURNAL

DATE:		TIME:		SEASON:	○ SPRING ○ SUMMER ○ FALL ○ WINTER
WEATHER CONDITIONS:		○ HOT ○ WARM ○ SUNNY ○ CLOUDY ○ RAINY ○ WINDY ○ FOGGY ○ COLD				
BUG NAME:					
WHERE DID YOU FIND IT?					
WHAT COLOR(S) IS THE BUG?					
NUMBER OF LEGS?		**DOES IT HAVE WINGS?**		○ YES ○ NO ○ NOT SURE	
NUMBER OF LEGS?					
THE BUG IS...		○ BIG ○ SHINY ○ FAST ○ SCARY ○ LITTLE ○ SLOW ○ CUTE ○ ROUND ○ THIN			
DOES IT MAKE ANY SOUND?		○ YES ○ NO	**WAS IT ALONE OR IN A GROUP?**	○ ALONE ○ GROUP	

NOTES

PHOTO/DRAWING

BUG JOURNAL

DATE:		TIME:		SEASON:	○ SPRING ○ SUMMER ○ FALL ○ WINTER
WEATHER CONDITIONS:			○ HOT ○ WARM ○ SUNNY ○ CLOUDY ○ RAINY ○ WINDY ○ FOGGY ○ COLD		
BUG NAME:					
WHERE DID YOU FIND IT?					
WHAT COLOR(S) IS THE BUG?					
NUMBER OF LEGS?		**DOES IT HAVE WINGS?**		○ YES ○ NO ○ NOT SURE	
NUMBER OF LEGS?					
THE BUG IS...		○ BIG ○ SHINY ○ FAST ○ SCARY ○ LITTLE ○ SLOW ○ CUTE ○ ROUND ○ THIN			
DOES IT MAKE ANY SOUND?	○ YES ○ NO	**WAS IT ALONE OR IN A GROUP?**		○ ALONE ○ GROUP	

NOTES

PHOTO/DRAWING

BUG JOURNAL

DATE:		TIME:		SEASON:	○ SPRING ○ SUMMER ○ FALL ○ WINTER	

WEATHER CONDITIONS:	○ HOT ○ WARM ○ SUNNY ○ CLOUDY ○ RAINY ○ WINDY ○ FOGGY ○ COLD
BUG NAME:	
WHERE DID YOU FIND IT?	
WHAT COLOR(S) IS THE BUG?	

NUMBER OF LEGS?		DOES IT HAVE WINGS?	○ YES ○ NO ○ NOT SURE
NUMBER OF LEGS?			

THE BUG IS…	○ BIG ○ SHINY ○ FAST ○ SCARY ○ LITTLE ○ SLOW ○ CUTE ○ ROUND ○ THIN

DOES IT MAKE ANY SOUND?	○ YES ○ NO	WAS IT ALONE OR IN A GROUP?	○ ALONE ○ GROUP

NOTES

PHOTO/DRAWING

BUG JOURNAL

DATE:		TIME:		SEASON:	○ SPRING ○ SUMMER ○ FALL ○ WINTER
WEATHER CONDITIONS:			○ HOT ○ WARM ○ SUNNY ○ CLOUDY ○ RAINY ○ WINDY ○ FOGGY ○ COLD		
BUG NAME:					
WHERE DID YOU FIND IT?					
WHAT COLOR(S) IS THE BUG?					
NUMBER OF LEGS?			**DOES IT HAVE WINGS?**	○ YES ○ NO ○ NOT SURE	
NUMBER OF LEGS?					
THE BUG IS...		○ BIG ○ SHINY ○ FAST ○ SCARY ○ LITTLE ○ SLOW ○ CUTE ○ ROUND ○ THIN			
DOES IT MAKE ANY SOUND?	○ YES ○ NO		**WAS IT ALONE OR IN A GROUP?**	○ ALONE ○ GROUP	

NOTES

PHOTO/DRAWING

BUG JOURNAL

DATE:		TIME:		SEASON:	○ SPRING ○ SUMMER ○ FALL ○ WINTER
WEATHER CONDITIONS:		○ HOT ○ WARM ○ SUNNY ○ CLOUDY ○ RAINY ○ WINDY ○ FOGGY ○ COLD			
BUG NAME:					
WHERE DID YOU FIND IT?					
WHAT COLOR(S) IS THE BUG?					
NUMBER OF LEGS?		**DOES IT HAVE WINGS?**		○ YES ○ NO ○ NOT SURE	
NUMBER OF LEGS?					
THE BUG IS…	○ BIG ○ SHINY ○ FAST ○ SCARY ○ LITTLE ○ SLOW ○ CUTE ○ ROUND ○ THIN				
DOES IT MAKE ANY SOUND?	○ YES ○ NO	**WAS IT ALONE OR IN A GROUP?**			○ ALONE ○ GROUP

NOTES

PHOTO/DRAWING

BUG JOURNAL

DATE:		TIME:		SEASON:	○ SPRING ○ SUMMER ○ FALL ○ WINTER
WEATHER CONDITIONS:			○ HOT ○ WARM ○ SUNNY ○ CLOUDY ○ RAINY ○ WINDY ○ FOGGY ○ COLD		
BUG NAME:					
WHERE DID YOU FIND IT?					
WHAT COLOR(S) IS THE BUG?					
NUMBER OF LEGS?		**DOES IT HAVE WINGS?**		○ YES ○ NO ○ NOT SURE	
NUMBER OF LEGS?					
THE BUG IS...		○ BIG ○ SHINY ○ FAST ○ SCARY ○ LITTLE ○ SLOW ○ CUTE ○ ROUND ○ THIN			
DOES IT MAKE ANY SOUND?	○ YES ○ NO	**WAS IT ALONE OR IN A GROUP?**		○ ALONE ○ GROUP	

NOTES

PHOTO/DRAWING

BUG JOURNAL

DATE:		TIME:		SEASON:	○ SPRING ○ SUMMER ○ FALL ○ WINTER
WEATHER CONDITIONS:		○ HOT ○ WARM ○ SUNNY ○ CLOUDY ○ RAINY ○ WINDY ○ FOGGY ○ COLD			
BUG NAME:					
WHERE DID YOU FIND IT?					
WHAT COLOR(S) IS THE BUG?					
NUMBER OF LEGS?		DOES IT HAVE WINGS?	○ YES ○ NO ○ NOT SURE		
NUMBER OF LEGS?					
THE BUG IS...	○ BIG ○ SHINY ○ FAST ○ SCARY ○ LITTLE ○ SLOW ○ CUTE ○ ROUND ○ THIN				
DOES IT MAKE ANY SOUND?	○ YES ○ NO	WAS IT ALONE OR IN A GROUP?	○ ALONE ○ GROUP		

NOTES

PHOTO/DRAWING

BUG JOURNAL

DATE:		TIME:		SEASON:	○ SPRING ○ SUMMER ○ FALL ○ WINTER
WEATHER CONDITIONS:		○ HOT ○ WARM ○ SUNNY ○ CLOUDY ○ RAINY ○ WINDY ○ FOGGY ○ COLD
BUG NAME:		
WHERE DID YOU FIND IT?		
WHAT COLOR(S) IS THE BUG?		
NUMBER OF LEGS?			DOES IT HAVE WINGS?		○ YES ○ NO ○ NOT SURE
NUMBER OF LEGS?		
THE BUG IS…		○ BIG ○ SHINY ○ FAST ○ SCARY ○ LITTLE ○ SLOW ○ CUTE ○ ROUND ○ THIN
DOES IT MAKE ANY SOUND?	○ YES ○ NO		WAS IT ALONE OR IN A GROUP?		○ ALONE ○ GROUP

NOTES

PHOTO/DRAWING

BUG JOURNAL

DATE:		TIME:		SEASON:	○ SPRING ○ SUMMER ○ FALL ○ WINTER	
WEATHER CONDITIONS:		○ HOT ○ WARM ○ SUNNY ○ CLOUDY ○ RAINY ○ WINDY ○ FOGGY ○ COLD				
BUG NAME:						
WHERE DID YOU FIND IT?						
WHAT COLOR(S) IS THE BUG?						
NUMBER OF LEGS?			DOES IT HAVE WINGS?		○ YES ○ NO ○ NOT SURE	
NUMBER OF LEGS?						
THE BUG IS...		○ BIG ○ SHINY ○ FAST ○ SCARY ○ LITTLE ○ SLOW ○ CUTE ○ ROUND ○ THIN				
DOES IT MAKE ANY SOUND?		○ YES ○ NO	WAS IT ALONE OR IN A GROUP?		○ ALONE ○ GROUP	

NOTES

PHOTO/DRAWING

BUG JOURNAL

DATE:		TIME:		SEASON:	○ SPRING ○ SUMMER ○ FALL ○ WINTER	
WEATHER CONDITIONS:		○ HOT ○ WARM ○ SUNNY ○ CLOUDY ○ RAINY ○ WINDY ○ FOGGY ○ COLD				
BUG NAME:						
WHERE DID YOU FIND IT?						
WHAT COLOR(S) IS THE BUG?						
NUMBER OF LEGS?			DOES IT HAVE WINGS?		○ YES ○ NO ○ NOT SURE	
NUMBER OF LEGS?						
THE BUG IS...		○ BIG ○ SHINY ○ FAST ○ SCARY ○ LITTLE ○ SLOW ○ CUTE ○ ROUND ○ THIN				
DOES IT MAKE ANY SOUND?	○ YES ○ NO		WAS IT ALONE OR IN A GROUP?		○ ALONE ○ GROUP	

NOTES

PHOTO/DRAWING

BUG JOURNAL

DATE:		TIME:		SEASON:	○ SPRING ○ SUMMER ○ FALL ○ WINTER
WEATHER CONDITIONS:		○ HOT ○ WARM ○ SUNNY ○ CLOUDY ○ RAINY ○ WINDY ○ FOGGY ○ COLD
BUG NAME:					
WHERE DID YOU FIND IT?					
WHAT COLOR(S) IS THE BUG?					
NUMBER OF LEGS?		**DOES IT HAVE WINGS?**		○ YES ○ NO ○ NOT SURE	
NUMBER OF LEGS?					
THE BUG IS...	○ BIG ○ SHINY ○ FAST ○ SCARY ○ LITTLE ○ SLOW ○ CUTE ○ ROUND ○ THIN				
DOES IT MAKE ANY SOUND?	○ YES ○ NO	**WAS IT ALONE OR IN A GROUP?**		○ ALONE ○ GROUP	

NOTES

PHOTO/DRAWING

BUG JOURNAL

DATE:		TIME:		SEASON:	○ SPRING ○ SUMMER ○ FALL ○ WINTER	
WEATHER CONDITIONS:		○ HOT ○ WARM ○ SUNNY ○ CLOUDY ○ RAINY ○ WINDY ○ FOGGY ○ COLD				
BUG NAME:						
WHERE DID YOU FIND IT?						
WHAT COLOR(S) IS THE BUG?						
NUMBER OF LEGS?			DOES IT HAVE WINGS?		○ YES ○ NO ○ NOT SURE	
NUMBER OF LEGS?						
THE BUG IS...		○ BIG ○ SHINY ○ FAST ○ SCARY ○ LITTLE ○ SLOW ○ CUTE ○ ROUND ○ THIN				
DOES IT MAKE ANY SOUND?	○ YES ○ NO		WAS IT ALONE OR IN A GROUP?		○ ALONE ○ GROUP	

NOTES

PHOTO/DRAWING

BUG JOURNAL

DATE:		TIME:		SEASON:	○ SPRING ○ SUMMER ○ FALL ○ WINTER
WEATHER CONDITIONS:			○ HOT ○ WARM ○ SUNNY ○ CLOUDY ○ RAINY ○ WINDY ○ FOGGY ○ COLD
BUG NAME:					
WHERE DID YOU FIND IT?					
WHAT COLOR(S) IS THE BUG?					
NUMBER OF LEGS?			**DOES IT HAVE WINGS?**		○ YES ○ NO ○ NOT SURE
NUMBER OF LEGS?					
THE BUG IS...		○ BIG ○ SHINY ○ FAST ○ SCARY ○ LITTLE ○ SLOW ○ CUTE ○ ROUND ○ THIN
DOES IT MAKE ANY SOUND?		○ YES ○ NO	**WAS IT ALONE OR IN A GROUP?**		○ ALONE ○ GROUP

NOTES

PHOTO/DRAWING

BUG JOURNAL

DATE:		TIME:		SEASON:	○ SPRING ○ SUMMER ○ FALL ○ WINTER
WEATHER CONDITIONS:			○ HOT ○ WARM ○ SUNNY ○ CLOUDY ○ RAINY ○ WINDY ○ FOGGY ○ COLD
BUG NAME:					
WHERE DID YOU FIND IT?					
WHAT COLOR(S) IS THE BUG?					
NUMBER OF LEGS?			**DOES IT HAVE WINGS?**		○ YES ○ NO ○ NOT SURE
NUMBER OF LEGS?					
THE BUG IS...		○ BIG ○ SHINY ○ FAST ○ SCARY ○ LITTLE ○ SLOW ○ CUTE ○ ROUND ○ THIN
DOES IT MAKE ANY SOUND?		○ YES ○ NO	**WAS IT ALONE OR IN A GROUP?**		○ ALONE ○ GROUP

NOTES

PHOTO/DRAWING

BUG JOURNAL

DATE:		TIME:		SEASON:	○ SPRING ○ SUMMER ○ FALL ○ WINTER
WEATHER CONDITIONS:			○ HOT ○ WARM ○ SUNNY ○ CLOUDY ○ RAINY ○ WINDY ○ FOGGY ○ COLD		
BUG NAME:					
WHERE DID YOU FIND IT?					
WHAT COLOR(S) IS THE BUG?					
NUMBER OF LEGS?		**DOES IT HAVE WINGS?**		○ YES ○ NO ○ NOT SURE	
NUMBER OF LEGS?					
THE BUG IS...		○ BIG ○ SHINY ○ FAST ○ SCARY ○ LITTLE ○ SLOW ○ CUTE ○ ROUND ○ THIN			
DOES IT MAKE ANY SOUND?	○ YES ○ NO	**WAS IT ALONE OR IN A GROUP?**		○ ALONE ○ GROUP	

NOTES

PHOTO/DRAWING

BUG JOURNAL

DATE:		TIME:		SEASON:	○ SPRING ○ SUMMER ○ FALL ○ WINTER
WEATHER CONDITIONS:		○ HOT ○ WARM ○ SUNNY ○ CLOUDY ○ RAINY ○ WINDY ○ FOGGY ○ COLD
BUG NAME:					
WHERE DID YOU FIND IT?					
WHAT COLOR(S) IS THE BUG?					
NUMBER OF LEGS?		DOES IT HAVE WINGS?		○ YES ○ NO ○ NOT SURE	
NUMBER OF LEGS?					
THE BUG IS…		○ BIG ○ SHINY ○ FAST ○ SCARY ○ LITTLE ○ SLOW ○ CUTE ○ ROUND ○ THIN
DOES IT MAKE ANY SOUND?	○ YES ○ NO	WAS IT ALONE OR IN A GROUP?		○ ALONE ○ GROUP	

NOTES

PHOTO/DRAWING

BUG JOURNAL

DATE:		TIME:		SEASON:	○ SPRING ○ SUMMER ○ FALL ○ WINTER
WEATHER CONDITIONS:		○ HOT ○ WARM ○ SUNNY ○ CLOUDY ○ RAINY ○ WINDY ○ FOGGY ○ COLD
BUG NAME:					
WHERE DID YOU FIND IT?					
WHAT COLOR(S) IS THE BUG?					
NUMBER OF LEGS?		**DOES IT HAVE WINGS?**		○ YES ○ NO ○ NOT SURE	
NUMBER OF LEGS?					
THE BUG IS...		○ BIG ○ SHINY ○ FAST ○ SCARY ○ LITTLE ○ SLOW ○ CUTE ○ ROUND ○ THIN
DOES IT MAKE ANY SOUND?	○ YES ○ NO	**WAS IT ALONE OR IN A GROUP?**		○ ALONE ○ GROUP	

NOTES

PHOTO/DRAWING

BUG JOURNAL

DATE:		TIME:		SEASON:	○ SPRING ○ SUMMER ○ FALL ○ WINTER
WEATHER CONDITIONS:			○ HOT ○ WARM ○ SUNNY ○ CLOUDY ○ RAINY ○ WINDY ○ FOGGY ○ COLD		
BUG NAME:					
WHERE DID YOU FIND IT?					
WHAT COLOR(S) IS THE BUG?					
NUMBER OF LEGS?			**DOES IT HAVE WINGS?**		○ YES ○ NO ○ NOT SURE
NUMBER OF LEGS?					
THE BUG IS...			○ BIG ○ SHINY ○ FAST ○ SCARY ○ LITTLE ○ SLOW ○ CUTE ○ ROUND ○ THIN		
DOES IT MAKE ANY SOUND?	○ YES ○ NO		**WAS IT ALONE OR IN A GROUP?**		○ ALONE ○ GROUP

NOTES

PHOTO/DRAWING

BUG JOURNAL

DATE:		TIME:		SEASON:	○ SPRING ○ SUMMER ○ FALL ○ WINTER
WEATHER CONDITIONS:		○ HOT ○ WARM ○ SUNNY ○ CLOUDY ○ RAINY ○ WINDY ○ FOGGY ○ COLD
BUG NAME:					
WHERE DID YOU FIND IT?					
WHAT COLOR(S) IS THE BUG?					
NUMBER OF LEGS?		**DOES IT HAVE WINGS?**		○ YES ○ NO ○ NOT SURE	
NUMBER OF LEGS?					
THE BUG IS...		○ BIG ○ SHINY ○ FAST ○ SCARY ○ LITTLE ○ SLOW ○ CUTE ○ ROUND ○ THIN
DOES IT MAKE ANY SOUND?	○ YES ○ NO	**WAS IT ALONE OR IN A GROUP?**		○ ALONE ○ GROUP	

NOTES

PHOTO/DRAWING

BUG JOURNAL

DATE:		TIME:		SEASON:	○ SPRING ○ SUMMER ○ FALL ○ WINTER	
WEATHER CONDITIONS:		○ HOT ○ WARM ○ SUNNY ○ CLOUDY ○ RAINY ○ WINDY ○ FOGGY ○ COLD				
BUG NAME:						
WHERE DID YOU FIND IT?						
WHAT COLOR(S) IS THE BUG?						
NUMBER OF LEGS?			DOES IT HAVE WINGS?		○ YES ○ NO ○ NOT SURE	
NUMBER OF LEGS?						
THE BUG IS...		○ BIG ○ SHINY ○ FAST ○ SCARY ○ LITTLE ○ SLOW ○ CUTE ○ ROUND ○ THIN				
DOES IT MAKE ANY SOUND?		○ YES ○ NO	WAS IT ALONE OR IN A GROUP?		○ ALONE ○ GROUP	

NOTES

PHOTO/DRAWING

BUG JOURNAL

DATE:		TIME:		SEASON:	○ SPRING ○ SUMMER ○ FALL ○ WINTER	
WEATHER CONDITIONS:		○ HOT ○ WARM ○ SUNNY ○ CLOUDY ○ RAINY ○ WINDY ○ FOGGY ○ COLD				
BUG NAME:						
WHERE DID YOU FIND IT?						
WHAT COLOR(S) IS THE BUG?						
NUMBER OF LEGS?			DOES IT HAVE WINGS?		○ YES ○ NO ○ NOT SURE	
NUMBER OF LEGS?						
THE BUG IS...		○ BIG ○ SHINY ○ FAST ○ SCARY ○ LITTLE ○ SLOW ○ CUTE ○ ROUND ○ THIN				
DOES IT MAKE ANY SOUND?		○ YES ○ NO	WAS IT ALONE OR IN A GROUP?		○ ALONE ○ GROUP	

NOTES

PHOTO/DRAWING

BUG JOURNAL

DATE:		TIME:		SEASON:	○ SPRING ○ SUMMER ○ FALL ○ WINTER	
WEATHER CONDITIONS:		○ HOT ○ WARM ○ SUNNY ○ CLOUDY ○ RAINY ○ WINDY ○ FOGGY ○ COLD				
BUG NAME:						
WHERE DID YOU FIND IT?						
WHAT COLOR(S) IS THE BUG?						
NUMBER OF LEGS?			DOES IT HAVE WINGS?		○ YES ○ NO ○ NOT SURE	
NUMBER OF LEGS?						
THE BUG IS…		○ BIG ○ SHINY ○ FAST ○ SCARY ○ LITTLE ○ SLOW ○ CUTE ○ ROUND ○ THIN				
DOES IT MAKE ANY SOUND?		○ YES ○ NO		WAS IT ALONE OR IN A GROUP?	○ ALONE ○ GROUP	

NOTES

PHOTO/DRAWING

BUG JOURNAL

DATE:		TIME:		SEASON:	○ SPRING ○ SUMMER ○ FALL ○ WINTER
WEATHER CONDITIONS:		○ HOT ○ WARM ○ SUNNY ○ CLOUDY ○ RAINY ○ WINDY ○ FOGGY ○ COLD
BUG NAME:					
WHERE DID YOU FIND IT?					
WHAT COLOR(S) IS THE BUG?					
NUMBER OF LEGS?		**DOES IT HAVE WINGS?**		○ YES ○ NO ○ NOT SURE	
NUMBER OF LEGS?					
THE BUG IS...		○ BIG ○ SHINY ○ FAST ○ SCARY ○ LITTLE ○ SLOW ○ CUTE ○ ROUND ○ THIN			
DOES IT MAKE ANY SOUND?	○ YES ○ NO	**WAS IT ALONE OR IN A GROUP?**		○ ALONE ○ GROUP	

NOTES

PHOTO/DRAWING

BUG JOURNAL

DATE:		TIME:		SEASON:	○ SPRING ○ SUMMER ○ FALL ○ WINTER
WEATHER CONDITIONS:		○ HOT ○ WARM ○ SUNNY ○ CLOUDY ○ RAINY ○ WINDY ○ FOGGY ○ COLD				
BUG NAME:					
WHERE DID YOU FIND IT?					
WHAT COLOR(S) IS THE BUG?					
NUMBER OF LEGS?		DOES IT HAVE WINGS?		○ YES ○ NO ○ NOT SURE	
NUMBER OF LEGS?					
THE BUG IS...		○ BIG ○ SHINY ○ FAST ○ SCARY ○ LITTLE ○ SLOW ○ CUTE ○ ROUND ○ THIN				
DOES IT MAKE ANY SOUND?	○ YES ○ NO	WAS IT ALONE OR IN A GROUP?			○ ALONE ○ GROUP

NOTES

PHOTO/DRAWING

BUG JOURNAL

DATE:		TIME:		SEASON:	○ SPRING ○ SUMMER ○ FALL ○ WINTER
WEATHER CONDITIONS:			○ HOT ○ WARM ○ SUNNY ○ CLOUDY ○ RAINY ○ WINDY ○ FOGGY ○ COLD
BUG NAME:					
WHERE DID YOU FIND IT?					
WHAT COLOR(S) IS THE BUG?					
NUMBER OF LEGS?		**DOES IT HAVE WINGS?**		○ YES ○ NO ○ NOT SURE	
NUMBER OF LEGS?					
THE BUG IS...		○ BIG ○ SHINY ○ FAST ○ SCARY ○ LITTLE ○ SLOW ○ CUTE ○ ROUND ○ THIN
DOES IT MAKE ANY SOUND?	○ YES ○ NO	**WAS IT ALONE OR IN A GROUP?**		○ ALONE ○ GROUP	

NOTES

PHOTO/DRAWING

BUG JOURNAL

DATE:		TIME:		SEASON:	○ SPRING ○ SUMMER ○ FALL ○ WINTER
WEATHER CONDITIONS:			○ HOT ○ WARM ○ SUNNY ○ CLOUDY ○ RAINY ○ WINDY ○ FOGGY ○ COLD		
BUG NAME:					
WHERE DID YOU FIND IT?					
WHAT COLOR(S) IS THE BUG?					
NUMBER OF LEGS?		**DOES IT HAVE WINGS?**		○ YES ○ NO ○ NOT SURE	
NUMBER OF LEGS?					
THE BUG IS...		○ BIG ○ SHINY ○ FAST ○ SCARY ○ LITTLE ○ SLOW ○ CUTE ○ ROUND ○ THIN			
DOES IT MAKE ANY SOUND?	○ YES ○ NO	**WAS IT ALONE OR IN A GROUP?**		○ ALONE ○ GROUP	

NOTES

PHOTO/DRAWING

BUG JOURNAL

DATE:		TIME:		SEASON:	○ SPRING ○ SUMMER ○ FALL ○ WINTER

WEATHER CONDITIONS:	○ HOT ○ WARM ○ SUNNY ○ CLOUDY ○ RAINY ○ WINDY ○ FOGGY ○ COLD
BUG NAME:	
WHERE DID YOU FIND IT?	
WHAT COLOR(S) IS THE BUG?	

NUMBER OF LEGS?		DOES IT HAVE WINGS?	○ YES ○ NO ○ NOT SURE
NUMBER OF LEGS?			
THE BUG IS...	○ BIG ○ SHINY ○ FAST ○ SCARY ○ LITTLE ○ SLOW ○ CUTE ○ ROUND ○ THIN		
DOES IT MAKE ANY SOUND?	○ YES ○ NO	WAS IT ALONE OR IN A GROUP?	○ ALONE ○ GROUP

NOTES

PHOTO/DRAWING

BUG JOURNAL

DATE:		TIME:		SEASON:	○ SPRING ○ SUMMER ○ FALL ○ WINTER	
WEATHER CONDITIONS:		○ HOT ○ WARM ○ SUNNY ○ CLOUDY ○ RAINY ○ WINDY ○ FOGGY ○ COLD				
BUG NAME:						
WHERE DID YOU FIND IT?						
WHAT COLOR(S) IS THE BUG?						
NUMBER OF LEGS?			DOES IT HAVE WINGS?		○ YES ○ NO ○ NOT SURE	
NUMBER OF LEGS?						
THE BUG IS...		○ BIG ○ SHINY ○ FAST ○ SCARY ○ LITTLE ○ SLOW ○ CUTE ○ ROUND ○ THIN				
DOES IT MAKE ANY SOUND?		○ YES ○ NO	WAS IT ALONE OR IN A GROUP?		○ ALONE ○ GROUP	

NOTES

PHOTO/DRAWING

BUG JOURNAL

DATE:		TIME:		SEASON:	○ SPRING ○ SUMMER ○ FALL ○ WINTER

WEATHER CONDITIONS:	○ HOT ○ WARM ○ SUNNY ○ CLOUDY ○ RAINY ○ WINDY ○ FOGGY ○ COLD
BUG NAME:	
WHERE DID YOU FIND IT?	
WHAT COLOR(S) IS THE BUG?	

NUMBER OF LEGS?		DOES IT HAVE WINGS?	○ YES ○ NO ○ NOT SURE

NUMBER OF LEGS?	
THE BUG IS...	○ BIG ○ SHINY ○ FAST ○ SCARY ○ LITTLE ○ SLOW ○ CUTE ○ ROUND ○ THIN

DOES IT MAKE ANY SOUND?	○ YES ○ NO	WAS IT ALONE OR IN A GROUP?	○ ALONE ○ GROUP

NOTES

PHOTO/DRAWING

BUG JOURNAL

DATE:		TIME:		SEASON:	○ SPRING ○ SUMMER ○ FALL ○ WINTER	
WEATHER CONDITIONS:		○ HOT ○ WARM ○ SUNNY ○ CLOUDY ○ RAINY ○ WINDY ○ FOGGY ○ COLD				
BUG NAME:						
WHERE DID YOU FIND IT?						
WHAT COLOR(S) IS THE BUG?						
NUMBER OF LEGS?		DOES IT HAVE WINGS?		○ YES ○ NO ○ NOT SURE		
NUMBER OF LEGS?						
THE BUG IS...		○ BIG ○ SHINY ○ FAST ○ SCARY ○ LITTLE ○ SLOW ○ CUTE ○ ROUND ○ THIN				
DOES IT MAKE ANY SOUND?	○ YES ○ NO	WAS IT ALONE OR IN A GROUP?		○ ALONE ○ GROUP		

NOTES

PHOTO/DRAWING

BUG JOURNAL

DATE:		TIME:		SEASON:	○ SPRING ○ SUMMER ○ FALL ○ WINTER
WEATHER CONDITIONS:					○ HOT ○ WARM ○ SUNNY ○ CLOUDY ○ RAINY ○ WINDY ○ FOGGY ○ COLD
BUG NAME:					
WHERE DID YOU FIND IT?					
WHAT COLOR(S) IS THE BUG?					
NUMBER OF LEGS?			**DOES IT HAVE WINGS?**		○ YES ○ NO ○ NOT SURE
NUMBER OF LEGS?					
THE BUG IS…					○ BIG ○ SHINY ○ FAST ○ SCARY ○ LITTLE ○ SLOW ○ CUTE ○ ROUND ○ THIN
DOES IT MAKE ANY SOUND?		○ YES ○ NO	**WAS IT ALONE OR IN A GROUP?**		○ ALONE ○ GROUP

NOTES

PHOTO/DRAWING

BUG JOURNAL

DATE:		TIME:		SEASON:	○ SPRING ○ SUMMER ○ FALL ○ WINTER
WEATHER CONDITIONS:		○ HOT ○ WARM ○ SUNNY ○ CLOUDY ○ RAINY ○ WINDY ○ FOGGY ○ COLD				
BUG NAME:						
WHERE DID YOU FIND IT?						
WHAT COLOR(S) IS THE BUG?						
NUMBER OF LEGS?		DOES IT HAVE WINGS?		○ YES ○ NO ○ NOT SURE	
NUMBER OF LEGS?						
THE BUG IS...		○ BIG ○ SHINY ○ FAST ○ SCARY ○ LITTLE ○ SLOW ○ CUTE ○ ROUND ○ THIN				
DOES IT MAKE ANY SOUND?	○ YES ○ NO	WAS IT ALONE OR IN A GROUP?			○ ALONE ○ GROUP

NOTES

PHOTO/DRAWING

BUG JOURNAL

DATE:		TIME:		SEASON:	○ SPRING ○ SUMMER ○ FALL ○ WINTER
WEATHER CONDITIONS:		○ HOT ○ WARM ○ SUNNY ○ CLOUDY ○ RAINY ○ WINDY ○ FOGGY ○ COLD			
BUG NAME:					
WHERE DID YOU FIND IT?					
WHAT COLOR(S) IS THE BUG?					
NUMBER OF LEGS?		**DOES IT HAVE WINGS?**		○ YES ○ NO ○ NOT SURE	
NUMBER OF LEGS?					
THE BUG IS…	○ BIG ○ SHINY ○ FAST ○ SCARY ○ LITTLE ○ SLOW ○ CUTE ○ ROUND ○ THIN				
DOES IT MAKE ANY SOUND?	○ YES ○ NO	**WAS IT ALONE OR IN A GROUP?**		○ ALONE ○ GROUP	

NOTES

PHOTO/DRAWING

BUG JOURNAL

DATE:		TIME:		SEASON:	○ SPRING ○ SUMMER ○ FALL ○ WINTER	
WEATHER CONDITIONS:		○ HOT ○ WARM ○ SUNNY ○ CLOUDY ○ RAINY ○ WINDY ○ FOGGY ○ COLD	
BUG NAME:						
WHERE DID YOU FIND IT?						
WHAT COLOR(S) IS THE BUG?						
NUMBER OF LEGS?			DOES IT HAVE WINGS?		○ YES ○ NO ○ NOT SURE	
NUMBER OF LEGS?						
THE BUG IS...		○ BIG ○ SHINY ○ FAST ○ SCARY ○ LITTLE ○ SLOW ○ CUTE ○ ROUND ○ THIN				
DOES IT MAKE ANY SOUND?	○ YES ○ NO		WAS IT ALONE OR IN A GROUP?		○ ALONE ○ GROUP	

NOTES

PHOTO/DRAWING

BUG JOURNAL

DATE:		TIME:		SEASON:	○ SPRING ○ SUMMER ○ FALL ○ WINTER	
WEATHER CONDITIONS:		○ HOT ○ WARM ○ SUNNY ○ CLOUDY ○ RAINY ○ WINDY ○ FOGGY ○ COLD				
BUG NAME:						
WHERE DID YOU FIND IT?						
WHAT COLOR(S) IS THE BUG?						
NUMBER OF LEGS?			DOES IT HAVE WINGS?		○ YES ○ NO ○ NOT SURE	
NUMBER OF LEGS?						
THE BUG IS...		○ BIG ○ SHINY ○ FAST ○ SCARY ○ LITTLE ○ SLOW ○ CUTE ○ ROUND ○ THIN				
DOES IT MAKE ANY SOUND?		○ YES ○ NO	WAS IT ALONE OR IN A GROUP?		○ ALONE ○ GROUP	

NOTES

PHOTO/DRAWING

BUG JOURNAL

DATE:		TIME:		SEASON:	○ SPRING ○ SUMMER ○ FALL ○ WINTER	
WEATHER CONDITIONS:		○ HOT ○ WARM ○ SUNNY ○ CLOUDY ○ RAINY ○ WINDY ○ FOGGY ○ COLD				
BUG NAME:						
WHERE DID YOU FIND IT?						
WHAT COLOR(S) IS THE BUG?						
NUMBER OF LEGS?			DOES IT HAVE WINGS?		○ YES ○ NO ○ NOT SURE	
NUMBER OF LEGS?						
THE BUG IS…		○ BIG ○ SHINY ○ FAST ○ SCARY ○ LITTLE ○ SLOW ○ CUTE ○ ROUND ○ THIN				
DOES IT MAKE ANY SOUND?		○ YES ○ NO	WAS IT ALONE OR IN A GROUP?		○ ALONE ○ GROUP	

NOTES

PHOTO/DRAWING

BUG JOURNAL

DATE:		TIME:		SEASON:	○ SPRING ○ SUMMER ○ FALL ○ WINTER
WEATHER CONDITIONS:					○ HOT ○ WARM ○ SUNNY ○ CLOUDY ○ RAINY ○ WINDY ○ FOGGY ○ COLD

BUG NAME:	
WHERE DID YOU FIND IT?	
WHAT COLOR(S) IS THE BUG?	
NUMBER OF LEGS?		DOES IT HAVE WINGS?	○ YES ○ NO ○ NOT SURE
NUMBER OF LEGS?	
THE BUG IS...	○ BIG ○ SHINY ○ FAST ○ SCARY ○ LITTLE ○ SLOW ○ CUTE ○ ROUND ○ THIN
DOES IT MAKE ANY SOUND?	○ YES ○ NO	WAS IT ALONE OR IN A GROUP?	○ ALONE ○ GROUP

NOTES

PHOTO/DRAWING

BUG JOURNAL

DATE:		TIME:		SEASON:	○ SPRING ○ SUMMER ○ FALL ○ WINTER	
WEATHER CONDITIONS:		○ HOT ○ WARM ○ SUNNY ○ CLOUDY ○ RAINY ○ WINDY ○ FOGGY ○ COLD				
BUG NAME:						
WHERE DID YOU FIND IT?						
WHAT COLOR(S) IS THE BUG?						
NUMBER OF LEGS?			DOES IT HAVE WINGS?		○ YES ○ NO ○ NOT SURE	
NUMBER OF LEGS?						
THE BUG IS...		○ BIG ○ SHINY ○ FAST ○ SCARY ○ LITTLE ○ SLOW ○ CUTE ○ ROUND ○ THIN				
DOES IT MAKE ANY SOUND?		○ YES ○ NO	WAS IT ALONE OR IN A GROUP?		○ ALONE ○ GROUP	

NOTES

PHOTO/DRAWING

BUG JOURNAL

DATE:		TIME:		SEASON:	○ SPRING ○ SUMMER ○ FALL ○ WINTER
WEATHER CONDITIONS:		○ HOT ○ WARM ○ SUNNY ○ CLOUDY ○ RAINY ○ WINDY ○ FOGGY ○ COLD
BUG NAME:					
WHERE DID YOU FIND IT?					
WHAT COLOR(S) IS THE BUG?					
NUMBER OF LEGS?			DOES IT HAVE WINGS?	○ YES ○ NO ○ NOT SURE	
NUMBER OF LEGS?					
THE BUG IS...		○ BIG ○ SHINY ○ FAST ○ SCARY ○ LITTLE ○ SLOW ○ CUTE ○ ROUND ○ THIN
DOES IT MAKE ANY SOUND?	○ YES ○ NO		WAS IT ALONE OR IN A GROUP?	○ ALONE ○ GROUP	

NOTES

PHOTO/DRAWING

BUG JOURNAL

DATE:		TIME:		SEASON:	○ SPRING ○ SUMMER ○ FALL ○ WINTER
WEATHER CONDITIONS:		○ HOT ○ WARM ○ SUNNY ○ CLOUDY ○ RAINY ○ WINDY ○ FOGGY ○ COLD			
BUG NAME:					
WHERE DID YOU FIND IT?					
WHAT COLOR(S) IS THE BUG?					
NUMBER OF LEGS?		DOES IT HAVE WINGS?		○ YES ○ NO ○ NOT SURE	
NUMBER OF LEGS?					
THE BUG IS...		○ BIG ○ SHINY ○ FAST ○ SCARY ○ LITTLE ○ SLOW ○ CUTE ○ ROUND ○ THIN			
DOES IT MAKE ANY SOUND?	○ YES ○ NO	WAS IT ALONE OR IN A GROUP?		○ ALONE ○ GROUP	

NOTES

PHOTO/DRAWING

BUG JOURNAL

DATE:		TIME:		SEASON:	○ SPRING ○ SUMMER ○ FALL ○ WINTER
WEATHER CONDITIONS:					○ HOT ○ WARM ○ SUNNY ○ CLOUDY ○ RAINY ○ WINDY ○ FOGGY ○ COLD
BUG NAME:					
WHERE DID YOU FIND IT?					
WHAT COLOR(S) IS THE BUG?					
NUMBER OF LEGS?			**DOES IT HAVE WINGS?**		○ YES ○ NO ○ NOT SURE
NUMBER OF LEGS?					
THE BUG IS...			○ BIG ○ SHINY ○ FAST ○ SCARY ○ LITTLE ○ SLOW ○ CUTE ○ ROUND ○ THIN		
DOES IT MAKE ANY SOUND?		○ YES ○ NO	**WAS IT ALONE OR IN A GROUP?**		○ ALONE ○ GROUP

NOTES

PHOTO/DRAWING

BUG JOURNAL

DATE:		TIME:		SEASON:	○ SPRING ○ SUMMER ○ FALL ○ WINTER	
WEATHER CONDITIONS:			○ HOT ○ WARM ○ SUNNY ○ CLOUDY ○ RAINY ○ WINDY ○ FOGGY ○ COLD			
BUG NAME:						
WHERE DID YOU FIND IT?						
WHAT COLOR(S) IS THE BUG?						
NUMBER OF LEGS?			DOES IT HAVE WINGS?		○ YES ○ NO ○ NOT SURE	
NUMBER OF LEGS?						
THE BUG IS...		○ BIG ○ SHINY ○ FAST ○ SCARY ○ LITTLE ○ SLOW ○ CUTE ○ ROUND ○ THIN				
DOES IT MAKE ANY SOUND?	○ YES ○ NO		WAS IT ALONE OR IN A GROUP?		○ ALONE ○ GROUP	

NOTES

PHOTO/DRAWING

BUG JOURNAL

DATE:		TIME:		SEASON:	○ SPRING ○ SUMMER ○ FALL ○ WINTER
WEATHER CONDITIONS:			○ HOT ○ WARM ○ SUNNY ○ CLOUDY ○ RAINY ○ WINDY ○ FOGGY ○ COLD
BUG NAME:					
WHERE DID YOU FIND IT?					
WHAT COLOR(S) IS THE BUG?					
NUMBER OF LEGS?			**DOES IT HAVE WINGS?**		○ YES ○ NO ○ NOT SURE
NUMBER OF LEGS?					
THE BUG IS…			○ BIG ○ SHINY ○ FAST ○ SCARY ○ LITTLE ○ SLOW ○ CUTE ○ ROUND ○ THIN		
DOES IT MAKE ANY SOUND?		○ YES ○ NO	**WAS IT ALONE OR IN A GROUP?**		○ ALONE ○ GROUP

NOTES

PHOTO/DRAWING

BUG JOURNAL

DATE:		TIME:		SEASON:	○ SPRING ○ SUMMER ○ FALL ○ WINTER	
WEATHER CONDITIONS:			○ HOT ○ WARM ○ SUNNY ○ CLOUDY ○ RAINY ○ WINDY ○ FOGGY ○ COLD			
BUG NAME:						
WHERE DID YOU FIND IT?						
WHAT COLOR(S) IS THE BUG?						
NUMBER OF LEGS?			DOES IT HAVE WINGS?		○ YES ○ NO ○ NOT SURE	
NUMBER OF LEGS?						
THE BUG IS...			○ BIG ○ SHINY ○ FAST ○ SCARY ○ LITTLE ○ SLOW ○ CUTE ○ ROUND ○ THIN			
DOES IT MAKE ANY SOUND?		○ YES ○ NO	WAS IT ALONE OR IN A GROUP?		○ ALONE ○ GROUP	

NOTES

PHOTO/DRAWING

BUG JOURNAL

DATE:		TIME:		SEASON:	○ SPRING ○ SUMMER ○ FALL ○ WINTER
WEATHER CONDITIONS:		○ HOT ○ WARM ○ SUNNY ○ CLOUDY ○ RAINY ○ WINDY ○ FOGGY ○ COLD				
BUG NAME:						
WHERE DID YOU FIND IT?						
WHAT COLOR(S) IS THE BUG?						
NUMBER OF LEGS?		**DOES IT HAVE WINGS?**		○ YES ○ NO ○ NOT SURE	
NUMBER OF LEGS?						
THE BUG IS…	○ BIG ○ SHINY ○ FAST ○ SCARY ○ LITTLE ○ SLOW ○ CUTE ○ ROUND ○ THIN				
DOES IT MAKE ANY SOUND?	○ YES ○ NO	**WAS IT ALONE OR IN A GROUP?**	○ ALONE ○ GROUP	

NOTES

PHOTO/DRAWING

BUG JOURNAL

DATE:		TIME:		SEASON:	○ SPRING ○ SUMMER ○ FALL ○ WINTER
WEATHER CONDITIONS:			○ HOT ○ WARM ○ SUNNY ○ CLOUDY ○ RAINY ○ WINDY ○ FOGGY ○ COLD			
BUG NAME:						
WHERE DID YOU FIND IT?						
WHAT COLOR(S) IS THE BUG?						
NUMBER OF LEGS?			**DOES IT HAVE WINGS?**		○ YES ○ NO ○ NOT SURE
NUMBER OF LEGS?					
THE BUG IS...		○ BIG ○ SHINY ○ FAST ○ SCARY ○ LITTLE ○ SLOW ○ CUTE ○ ROUND ○ THIN				
DOES IT MAKE ANY SOUND?	○ YES ○ NO		**WAS IT ALONE OR IN A GROUP?**		○ ALONE ○ GROUP

NOTES

PHOTO/DRAWING

BUG JOURNAL

DATE:		TIME:		SEASON:	○ SPRING ○ SUMMER ○ FALL ○ WINTER
WEATHER CONDITIONS:		○ HOT ○ WARM ○ SUNNY ○ CLOUDY ○ RAINY ○ WINDY ○ FOGGY ○ COLD			
BUG NAME:					
WHERE DID YOU FIND IT?					
WHAT COLOR(S) IS THE BUG?					
NUMBER OF LEGS?		**DOES IT HAVE WINGS?**		○ YES ○ NO ○ NOT SURE	
NUMBER OF LEGS?					
THE BUG IS...	○ BIG ○ SHINY ○ FAST ○ SCARY ○ LITTLE ○ SLOW ○ CUTE ○ ROUND ○ THIN				
DOES IT MAKE ANY SOUND?	○ YES ○ NO	**WAS IT ALONE OR IN A GROUP?**			○ ALONE ○ GROUP

NOTES

PHOTO/DRAWING

BUG JOURNAL

DATE:		TIME:		SEASON:	○ SPRING ○ SUMMER ○ FALL ○ WINTER
WEATHER CONDITIONS:					○ HOT ○ WARM ○ SUNNY ○ CLOUDY ○ RAINY ○ WINDY ○ FOGGY ○ COLD
BUG NAME:					
WHERE DID YOU FIND IT?					
WHAT COLOR(S) IS THE BUG?					
NUMBER OF LEGS?			DOES IT HAVE WINGS?		○ YES ○ NO ○ NOT SURE
NUMBER OF LEGS?					
THE BUG IS...			○ BIG ○ SHINY ○ FAST ○ SCARY ○ LITTLE ○ SLOW ○ CUTE ○ ROUND ○ THIN		
DOES IT MAKE ANY SOUND?		○ YES ○ NO	WAS IT ALONE OR IN A GROUP?		○ ALONE ○ GROUP

NOTES

PHOTO/DRAWING

BUG JOURNAL

DATE:		TIME:		SEASON:	○ SPRING ○ SUMMER ○ FALL ○ WINTER	
WEATHER CONDITIONS:		○ HOT ○ WARM ○ SUNNY ○ CLOUDY ○ RAINY ○ WINDY ○ FOGGY ○ COLD				
BUG NAME:						
WHERE DID YOU FIND IT?						
WHAT COLOR(S) IS THE BUG?						
NUMBER OF LEGS?			DOES IT HAVE WINGS?		○ YES ○ NO ○ NOT SURE	
NUMBER OF LEGS?						
THE BUG IS...		○ BIG ○ SHINY ○ FAST ○ SCARY ○ LITTLE ○ SLOW ○ CUTE ○ ROUND ○ THIN				
DOES IT MAKE ANY SOUND?		○ YES ○ NO	WAS IT ALONE OR IN A GROUP?		○ ALONE ○ GROUP	

NOTES

PHOTO/DRAWING

BUG JOURNAL

DATE:		TIME:		SEASON:	○ SPRING ○ SUMMER ○ FALL ○ WINTER	
WEATHER CONDITIONS:		○ HOT ○ WARM ○ SUNNY ○ CLOUDY ○ RAINY ○ WINDY ○ FOGGY ○ COLD				
BUG NAME:						
WHERE DID YOU FIND IT?						
WHAT COLOR(S) IS THE BUG?						
NUMBER OF LEGS?			DOES IT HAVE WINGS?		○ YES ○ NO ○ NOT SURE	
NUMBER OF LEGS?						
THE BUG IS...		○ BIG ○ SHINY ○ FAST ○ SCARY ○ LITTLE ○ SLOW ○ CUTE ○ ROUND ○ THIN				
DOES IT MAKE ANY SOUND?	○ YES ○ NO	WAS IT ALONE OR IN A GROUP?			○ ALONE ○ GROUP	

NOTES

PHOTO/DRAWING

BUG JOURNAL

DATE:		TIME:		SEASON:	○ SPRING ○ SUMMER ○ FALL ○ WINTER
WEATHER CONDITIONS:			○ HOT ○ WARM ○ SUNNY ○ CLOUDY ○ RAINY ○ WINDY ○ FOGGY ○ COLD
BUG NAME:					
WHERE DID YOU FIND IT?					
WHAT COLOR(S) IS THE BUG?					
NUMBER OF LEGS?		**DOES IT HAVE WINGS?**		○ YES ○ NO ○ NOT SURE	
NUMBER OF LEGS?					
THE BUG IS...		○ BIG ○ SHINY ○ FAST ○ SCARY ○ LITTLE ○ SLOW ○ CUTE ○ ROUND ○ THIN
DOES IT MAKE ANY SOUND?	○ YES ○ NO	**WAS IT ALONE OR IN A GROUP?**		○ ALONE ○ GROUP	

NOTES

PHOTO/DRAWING

BUG JOURNAL

DATE:		TIME:		SEASON:	○ SPRING ○ SUMMER ○ FALL ○ WINTER
WEATHER CONDITIONS:					○ HOT ○ WARM ○ SUNNY ○ CLOUDY ○ RAINY ○ WINDY ○ FOGGY ○ COLD
BUG NAME:					
WHERE DID YOU FIND IT?					
WHAT COLOR(S) IS THE BUG?					
NUMBER OF LEGS?			**DOES IT HAVE WINGS?**		○ YES ○ NO ○ NOT SURE
NUMBER OF LEGS?					
THE BUG IS...			○ BIG ○ SHINY ○ FAST ○ SCARY ○ LITTLE ○ SLOW ○ CUTE ○ ROUND ○ THIN		
DOES IT MAKE ANY SOUND?	○ YES ○ NO		**WAS IT ALONE OR IN A GROUP?**		○ ALONE ○ GROUP

NOTES

PHOTO/DRAWING

BUG JOURNAL

DATE:		TIME:		SEASON:	○ SPRING ○ SUMMER ○ FALL ○ WINTER
WEATHER CONDITIONS:		○ HOT ○ WARM ○ SUNNY ○ CLOUDY ○ RAINY ○ WINDY ○ FOGGY ○ COLD
BUG NAME:					
WHERE DID YOU FIND IT?					
WHAT COLOR(S) IS THE BUG?					
NUMBER OF LEGS?		**DOES IT HAVE WINGS?**		○ YES ○ NO ○ NOT SURE	
NUMBER OF LEGS?					
THE BUG IS…		○ BIG ○ SHINY ○ FAST ○ SCARY ○ LITTLE ○ SLOW ○ CUTE ○ ROUND ○ THIN			
DOES IT MAKE ANY SOUND?	○ YES ○ NO	**WAS IT ALONE OR IN A GROUP?**		○ ALONE ○ GROUP	

NOTES

PHOTO/DRAWING

BUG JOURNAL

DATE:		TIME:		SEASON:	○ SPRING ○ SUMMER ○ FALL ○ WINTER
WEATHER CONDITIONS:			○ HOT ○ WARM ○ SUNNY ○ CLOUDY ○ RAINY ○ WINDY ○ FOGGY ○ COLD			
BUG NAME:					
WHERE DID YOU FIND IT?					
WHAT COLOR(S) IS THE BUG?					
NUMBER OF LEGS?		DOES IT HAVE WINGS?		○ YES ○ NO ○ NOT SURE	
NUMBER OF LEGS?					
THE BUG IS...		○ BIG ○ SHINY ○ FAST ○ SCARY ○ LITTLE ○ SLOW ○ CUTE ○ ROUND ○ THIN			
DOES IT MAKE ANY SOUND?	○ YES ○ NO	WAS IT ALONE OR IN A GROUP?		○ ALONE ○ GROUP	

NOTES

PHOTO/DRAWING

BUG JOURNAL

DATE:		TIME:		SEASON:	○ SPRING ○ SUMMER ○ FALL ○ WINTER	
WEATHER CONDITIONS:		○ HOT ○ WARM ○ SUNNY ○ CLOUDY ○ RAINY ○ WINDY ○ FOGGY ○ COLD				
BUG NAME:						
WHERE DID YOU FIND IT?						
WHAT COLOR(S) IS THE BUG?						
NUMBER OF LEGS?			DOES IT HAVE WINGS?		○ YES ○ NO ○ NOT SURE	
NUMBER OF LEGS?						
THE BUG IS...		○ BIG ○ SHINY ○ FAST ○ SCARY ○ LITTLE ○ SLOW ○ CUTE ○ ROUND ○ THIN				
DOES IT MAKE ANY SOUND?		○ YES ○ NO	WAS IT ALONE OR IN A GROUP?		○ ALONE ○ GROUP	

NOTES

PHOTO/DRAWING

BUG JOURNAL

DATE:		TIME:		SEASON:	○ SPRING ○ SUMMER ○ FALL ○ WINTER
WEATHER CONDITIONS:			○ HOT ○ WARM ○ SUNNY ○ CLOUDY ○ RAINY ○ WINDY ○ FOGGY ○ COLD		
BUG NAME:						
WHERE DID YOU FIND IT?						
WHAT COLOR(S) IS THE BUG?						
NUMBER OF LEGS?			**DOES IT HAVE WINGS?**		○ YES ○ NO ○ NOT SURE
NUMBER OF LEGS?						
THE BUG IS…		○ BIG ○ SHINY ○ FAST ○ SCARY ○ LITTLE ○ SLOW ○ CUTE ○ ROUND ○ THIN				
DOES IT MAKE ANY SOUND?	○ YES ○ NO	**WAS IT ALONE OR IN A GROUP?**		○ ALONE ○ GROUP	

NOTES

PHOTO/DRAWING

Printed in Great Britain
by Amazon